THE POET'S

TOOLBOX

Fur, Fangs, and Footprints

A Collection of Poems About Animals

Compiled and Annotated
by Patricia M. Stockland

Illustrated by
Sara Rojo Pérez

Compass Point Books
3109 West 50th Street, #115
Minneapolis, MN 55410

Visit Compass Point Books on the Internet at *www.compasspointbooks.com*
or e-mail your request to *custserv@compasspointbooks.com*

A special thank you to John, Elizabeth, and Chaneen

Permissions and Acknowledgements:
"Roger the Dog," 6. From: The Cat & the Cuckoo, published by Roaring Brook Press. Faber and Faber, Ltd., publishers. Copyright © 2002 by Ted Hughes. All rights reserved. "Cats," 7. Reprinted by permission of Harold Ober Associates Incorporated. Copyright © 1957 by Eleanor Farjeon. "Tiger," 8. "tiger" from ALL THE SMALL POEMS AND FOURTEEN by Valerie Worth. Copyright © 1987, 1994, by Valerie Worth. "The Tiger," 9. Printed by permission of Patricia M. Stockland. "Foal," 10. Printed by permission of the Isabel Bolton Estate. "My Horse, Fly Like a Bird," 11. Copyright © 1989 by Virginia Driving Hawk Sneve. Reprinted from DANCING TEEPEES by permission of Holiday House, Inc. "The Wolf," 12. Public domain. "Grandpa Bear's Lullaby," 13. Copyright © 1980 by Jane Yolen. First appeared in Dragon Night and Other Lullabies, published by Methuen. Reprinted by permission of Curtis Brown, Ltd. "The Camel's Complaint," 14. Public domain. "The Coyote," 16. "The Coyote" from MAMMALABILIA, copyright © 2000 by Douglas Florian, reprinted by permission of Harcourt, Inc. "The Platypus," 17. Every effort has been made to contact the author. Compass Point Books does not take credit for the authorship, ownership, or copyright of this poem. "The Hurt Doe," 18. Copyright © 1999 by Emanuel diPasquale. Used by permission of Marian Reiner for the author. "Chelsea," 19. Copyright © 1998 by James Stevenson. Used by permission of HarperCollins Publishers. "The Panther," 20. Copyright © 1940 by Ogden Nash, renewed. Reprinted by permissions of Curtis Brown, Ltd. "The Goat," 21. Public domain. "What They Said," 22. The Society of Authors as the Literary Representative of the Estate of Rose Fyleman. "Untitled," 23. Printed by permission of Ross Follett. "Pete at the Zoo," 24. Reprinted by consent of Brooks Permissions. "Just Three," 25. Copyright © 1971 by William Wise. First appeared in All on a Summer's Day, published by Pantheon. Reprinted by permission of Curtis Brown, Ltd.

Content Advisers: Jane Volkman, Patricia Kirkpatrick, Ph.D.
Rights Researcher: Nancy Loewen
Designer: The Design Lab

Library of Congress Cataloging-in-Publication Data
Fur, fangs, and footprints : a collection of animal poems / compiled and annotated
by Patricia M. Stockland.
p. cm. —- (The poet's toolbox)
Summary: An anthology of poems about animals, plus "Toolbox tips" that help the reader understand poetry
and how poems are written.
ISBN 0-7565-0562-3 (hardcover)
1. Animals—Juvenile poetry. 2. Poetry—Authorship—Juvenile literature. 3. Children's poetry, American.
(1. Animals—Poetry. 2. American poetry.) I. Stockland, Patricia M. II. Series.
PS595.A5F87 2004
808.81'9362—dc22   2003017103

Table of Contents

NOTE: In this book, words that are defined in the glossary are in **bold** the first time they appear in the text.

Open Your Toolbox

You've probably been to the zoo or had a pet, and you probably know that animals come in hundreds of different shapes and sizes. Sometimes, they're small and sweet. Other times, they're big, hairy, even scary! Almost everyone has a favorite animal. That animal might even be your best friend. How do you describe them—when you see a tiger hiding in the dark, or you get a dog you know you'll love for life, or you suspect your pet is thinking something and he just can't say it in words? Poetry can be a way to tell about those creatures—dogs, cats, horses, bears, elephants, mice, camels… even a platypus!

WHAT DOES POETRY DO?

Poetry helps energize your imagination. Poetry plays with words in ways you never imagined. Ordinary words are suddenly mysterious or exciting. Poetry opens your ears to different sounds—sentences can play like music. Everyone has smart ideas, and poetry can be a new language with which to share those ideas.

DOES A POET USE A TOOLBOX?

Poets use many different tools and materials to make their poems. Material poets use can be stuff that happens to them every day in their lives. Poets' tools are parts of speech (such as nouns, verbs, and adjectives), ways of writing (like different forms or types of poetry), and the interesting sounds that letters and words make when they're combined (like rhymes and repeated letters). This book will show you some different tools poets use to build poems, and it might even teach you to write some poetry.

HOW DOES THE POET'S TOOLBOX WORK?

First, read all the poems. After you read each one, take a look at the Toolbox Tip on the bottom of the page. These Toolbox Tips will help you understand a poetry tool the writer has used, or they might give you a hint about where the poet found the idea for that poem. Near the back of the book, you'll have the chance to begin using these tools yourself!

Roger the Dog

Asleep he wheezes at his ease.
He only wakes to scratch his fleas.

He hogs the fire, he bakes his head
As if it were a loaf of bread.

He's just a sack of snoring dog.
You can lug him like a log.

You can roll him with your foot,
He'll stay snoring where he's put.

I take him out for exercise,
He rolls in cowclap up to his eyes.

He will not race, he will not romp,
He saves his strength for gobble and
chomp.

He'll work as hard as you could wish
Emptying his dinner dish,

Then flops flat, and digs down deep,
Like a miner, into sleep.

—Ted Hughes

Dog tired

TOOLBOX TIP

DOG TIRED

Has your dog ever "baked his head as if it were a loaf of bread"? When you compare two different things using "as" or "like," you are using **similes.** They are a great way to compare things—and exaggerate.

Cats

Cats sleep
Anywhere,
Any table,
Any chair,
Top of piano,
Window-ledge,
In the middle,
On the edge,
Open drawer,
Empty shoe,
Anybody's
Lap will do,
Fitted in a
Cardboard box,
In the cupboard
With your frocks—
Anywhere!
They don't care!
Cats sleep
Anywhere.

—Eleanor Farjeon

TOOLBOX TIP

RHYME TIME

Words that end in the same sound are **rhymes.** They don't always have to be spelled the same, though. "Anywhere" and "chair" are rhymes. Can you find all of the rhymes on these pages?

Tiger

The tiger
Has swallowed
A black sun,

In his cold
Cage he
Carries it still:

Black flames
Flicker through
His fur,

Black rays roar
From the centers
Of his eyes.

—Valerie Worth

TOOLBOX TIP

THE SAME, BUT DIFFERENT

Poets use **metaphors** to suggest new and unusual ideas. A metaphor is an expression that gives the qualities of one thing to something else. Although the tiger hasn't really swallowed a black sun, what could the poet mean?

The tiger
Hides in the
Early evening...

Teeth and claws and fur
Invisible hunter
Gold and black stripes hide him
Every inch silently creeping, then suddenly
Roaring, he pounces

—Patricia M. Stockland

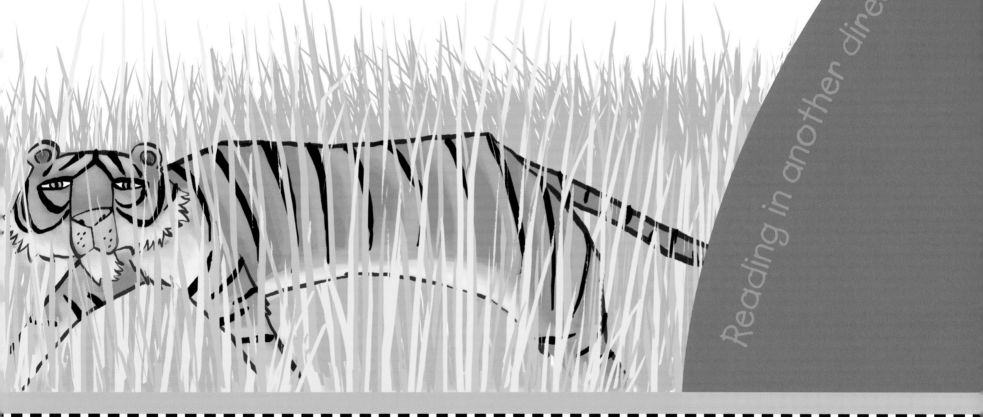

TOOLBOX TIP

READING IN ANOTHER DIRECTION

This poem is an **acrostic.** If you put the first letter of each line together, it will spell a word. Can you see the title of this poem?

Foal

Come trotting up
Beside your mother,
Little skinny.

Lay your neck across
Her back, and whinny,
Little foal.

You think you're a horse
Because you can trot—
But you're not.

Your eyes are so wild,
And each leg is as tall
As a pole;

And you're only a skittish
Child, after all,
Little foal.

—Mary Britton Miller

TOOLBOX TIP

A HORSE, OF COURSE
The picture you get in your mind when you read a
poem is **imagery.** Details like "wild," "tall," and
"little" help create imagery. Can you picture the foal?

A horse, of course

My Horse, Fly Like a Bird

My horse, fly like a bird
To carry me far
From the arrows of my enemies,
And I will tie red ribbons
To your streaming hair.

—Virginia Driving Hawk Sneve, adapted from a
   Lakota warrior's song to his horse

 TOOLBOX TIP

IN OTHER WORDS...

Poetry is popular in many different languages. This poem has been **translated** from Lakota, a Native American language. A translation changes a poem to mean the same thing in another language as it did in its original language.

The Wolf

When the pale moon hides and the wild wind wails,
And over the tree-tops the nighthawk sails,
The gray wolf sits on the world's far rim,
And howls: and it seems to comfort him.

The wolf is a lonely soul, you see,
No beast in the wood, nor bird in the tree,
But shuns his path; in the windy gloom
They give him plenty, and plenty of room.

So he sits with his long, lean face to the sky
Watching the ragged clouds go by.
There in the night, alone, apart,
Singing the song of his lone, wild heart.

Far away, on the world's dark rim
He howls, and it seems to comfort him.

—Georgia Roberts Durston

Musical poems

TOOLBOX TIP

MUSICAL POEMS

The beat of poetry that sometimes makes it feel like music is called **rhythm.** Sometimes rhymes create rhythm, and sometimes syllables, or beats, create it.

Grandpa Bear's Lullaby

The night is long
But fur is deep.
You will be warm
In winter sleep.

The food is gone
But dreams are sweet
And they will be
Your winter meat.

The cave is dark
But dreams are bright
And they will serve
As winter light.
Sleep, my little cubs, sleep.

—Jane Yolen

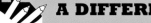

A DIFFERENT BEAT

TOOLBOX TIP Rhythm is measured in **meter**—this just means counting the beats in each line. Every line in this poem has the same number of beats— except one. Can you figure out how many beats are in each line?

The Camel's Complaint

Canary-birds feed on sugar and seed,
   Parrots have crackers to crunch;
And as for the poodles, they tell me the
   noodles
   Have chicken and cream for their
   lunch.
      But there's never a question
      About *my* digestion—
      Anything does for me.

Cats, you're aware, can repose in a chair,
   Chickens can roost upon rails;
Puppies are able to sleep in a stable,
   And oysters can slumber in pails.
      But no one supposes
      A poor camel dozes—
         Any place does for me.

Lambs are enclosed where it's never
   exposed,
   Coops are constructed for hens;
Kittens are treated to houses well
   heated,
   And pigs are protected by pens.
      But a camel comes handy
      Wherever it's sandy—
      Anywhere does for me.

People would laugh if you rode a giraffe,
   Or mounted the back of an ox;
It's nobody's habit to ride on a rabbit,
   Or try to bestraddle a fox.
      But as for a camel, he's
      Ridden by families—
         Any load does for me.

A snake is as round as a hole in the
   ground,
   And weasels are wavy and sleek;
And no alligator could ever be straighter
   Than lizards that live in a creek.
      But a camel's all lumpy
      And bumpy and humpy—
         Any shape does for me.

—Charles E. Carryl

Again, and again, and again . . .

and again, and again, and again . . .

TOOLBOX TIP

AGAIN, AND AGAIN, AND AGAIN . . .

Repetition is what happens when poets repeat certain words, phrases, or sounds. Repetition can help create **patterns.** Sometimes you need to repeat yourself and repeat yourself to make a point. What's the camel's point?

15

The Coyote

I prowl.
I growl.
My howl
Is throaty.
I love   o
A vowel,   o   o
For I am coyo   ote.

—Douglas Florian

TOOLBOX TIP

WHAT DO YOU SEE?
This **concrete poem** is a picture as well as a poem. That's
how concrete poems work! You can see the howl of the coyote.
Can you hear it? Say it aloud, and try to match the "o's."

The Platypus

The great platypus,
Swimming slowly through water,
Protecting its young.

—Gabriella Shaw

Grow up? No way!

TOOLBOX TIP

GROW UP? NO WAY!

Gabriella Shaw was 9 years old when she wrote this **haiku!** These poems are usually about nature or the seasons. They have 17 beats— five in the first and last lines and seven in the middle. Can you haiku?

The Hurt Doe

Four deer walk by my front yard this evening
One of the two does lingers behind
with a hurt leg. What can I do?
"Let it go; let it go,"
the grown-ups say
"It's the way of things."
But I worry.
What will happen to it?
Why can't I help?

—Emanuel diPasquale

A sad "tail"

TOOLBOX TIP

A SAD "TAIL"

Sometimes no tool is the best tool. These poets use **free verse**—poetry without any rhymes or patterns—to build their poems. How does free verse help to bring out the sadness of the stories?

18

Chelsea

Chelsea is gone.
Her water bowl is dry.
Her green collar lies in her empty dish.
The dog door that flapped when she
    went in and out is silent.

Beside her bed her teddy bear sits waiting.
In these last days
When we called Chelsea's name,
She hurt too much to come.
But we knew where she was
By the thumping of her tail on the floor.
And we could go to her
And kneel down
And put our arms around her.

—James Stevenson

The Panther

The panther is like a leopard,
Except it hasn't been peppered.
Should you behold a panther crouch,
Prepare to say Ouch.
Better yet, if called by a panther,
Don't anther.

—Ogden Nash

Are you kidding me?

20

TOOLBOX TIP

ARE YOU KIDDING ME?
Do you ever make up words or stories? Poets do. These poems might not make sense at first—they might make you laugh! Sometimes, that's the whole purpose of a poem.

The Goat

There was a man, now please take note,
There was a man, who had a goat.
He lov'd that goat, indeed he did,
He lov'd that goat, just like a kid.

One day that goat felt frisk and fine,
Ate three red shirts from off the line.
The man he grabbed him by the back,
And tied him to a railroad track.

But when the train hove into sight,
That goat grew pale and green with fright.
He heaved a sigh, as if in pain,
Coughed up those shirts and flagged the train.

—Author Unknown

TOOLBOX TIP

NOBODY KNOWS . . . !
You might know this poem as a song, but you still wouldn't know the poet.
Some poems have been around so long that no one knows where they
came from. Sometimes, the unknown author is called "anonymous."

21

What They Said

It's four o'clock,
Said the cock.

It's still dark,
Said the lark.

What's that?
Said the cat.

I want to sleep,
Said the sheep.

A bad habit,
Said the rabbit.

Of course,
Said the horse.

Let's have a spree,
Said the bee.

But where?
Said the hare.

In the barrow,
Said the sparrow.

I'm too big,
Said the pig.

In the house,
Said the mouse.

But the dog said —
Bow-wow,
It's too late now.

—German nursery rhyme
Translated by Rose Fyleman

TOOLBOX TIP

DID THEY REALLY SAY THAT?
Can animals really talk? They can in poetry thanks to **personification.**
The poets on these pages have given the animals the ability to talk. This
makes them seem more like people.

untitled

behave yourself
in my house
said the mouse
or here
you won't have cheese

just because
as you see
you're much bigger than me
doesn't mean
you can do
as you please

—Ross Follett

NO NAME?

Not all poets give titles to their poems. Sometimes
the poem is just listed as "untitled." Usually,
people will know the poem by its first line.

TOOLBOX TIP

Pete at the Zoo

I wonder if the elephant
Is lonely in his stall
When all the boys and girls are gone
And there's no shout at all,
And there's no one to stamp before
No one to note his might.
Does he hunch up, as I do,
Against the dark of night?

—Gwendolyn Brooks

TOOLBOX TIP

SEE A PATTERN?
Rhymes can create patterns in
poetry. Can you see which lines
rhyme to create a pattern?

Just Three

How very quiet things can be,
With just the dog, the cat, and me.
There's no one else to laugh and shout,
To dance and sing and run about.
With just the dog, the cat, and me,
How very quiet things can be.

—William Wise

Sit. Think. Stay.

TOOLBOX TIP

SIT. THINK. STAY.

Sometimes, quiet can make you think as much as action and sound can . . . . What do you hear in a quiet room? Is it really quiet? Thoughts you have when it's quiet might lead you to your own poetry!

THE POET'S

TOOLBOX

Collect Your Tools

Poets use a lot of tools to build their poems. These tools help to create different types of poems, like rhyming poems, free verse poems, acrostic poems, concrete poems, and even haikus. What poetry tools have you learned? When you find the answers to the questions on these pages, you're learning to work just like a poet. (Hint: Need help with a word you don't understand? Look in The Poet's Toolbox Glossary on page 28.)

1. When words end in the same sound, they **rhyme.** Find poems that have lines that rhyme at the end. Are the rhyming **patterns** always the same?

2. The poems on pages 18 and 19 are **free verse** poems—they don't use rhyming words or stick to set patterns. The poems sound like someone is just talking. These things make free verse poems different from rhyming poems. Can you find another poem that is a free verse poem?

3. In "The Camel's Complaint" (page 14), Charles E. Carryl separates groups of lines and ideas with **stanzas.** What are the five different things bothering the camel?

4. Animals can talk in poetry because of **personification.** How many poems can you find where the animal or animals are talking?

5. You read in "Roger the Dog" (page 6) that a dog can bake his head like a loaf of bread because of **similes.** Remember, similes make comparisons by saying one thing is like another. Find another poem that uses a simile.

Congratulations! Now you know a whole lot more about the tools poets use, and you're probably able to use some of these tools yourself. You've seen lots of examples. Now go to the next page, and get out your pencil and paper. It's time to build your own poems!

Now that you know how to use some poetry tools, it's time to go to work. Here's an activity that will help you get going on writing some of your own poems.

TAKE A POETRY FIELD TRIP

Take a poetry field trip to the zoo! It's a great place to find ideas for writing your own animal poems.

1. Get a notebook, something small that you can carry around the zoo. It can be a plain old notebook, nothing fancy.

2. Walk around with your friends and each find your favorite animal.

3. Watch the animal for awhile, and make a list of what the animal does—everything you can think of to notice.
   - What does the animal look like? Is it furry? Smooth? Rough-skinned? Dark? Light? Big? Small?
   - What does the animal eat? Meat? Vegetables? Grass? Bugs?
   - How does it smell?
   - How does it sound?
   - Where does it live? Are there other animals living with your favorite animal, or is it living alone?
   - Does the animal behave or look like a person? Look closely at its body parts—its facial features, legs, and paws (or claws!).

4. Now, become a poet. Read back over what you've written. Choose three entries that you really like—things you can really see and remember clearly. Then look at the poet's tools you practiced on the previous page. Try using some of those tools to turn your list into a poem about that animal. If you get stuck, just use one of the poems from the book as an example. "Pete at the Zoo" (page 24) might be useful if you are writing a rhyming poem. If you want to do an acrostic, check out "The Tiger" (page 9). At the end of the day, get together with your friends, and read the poems.

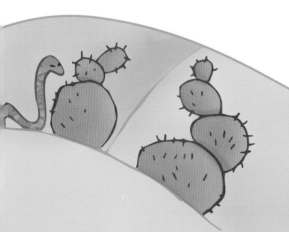

Go to Work

The Poet's Toolbox Glossary

The Poet's Toolbox Glossary can help you understand poetry tools used in this book and others in this series. Words in **color** are tools found in this book. Words in **black** are other poetry tools that will also be helpful as you work on your own poetry.

Acrostic poems use the first letters of each line to spell out a word, name, or phrase relating to the poem's topic.

Alliteration (ah-LIT-er-A-shun) is a tool that helps with sounds. It repeats consonant sounds or vowel sounds that are the same, like the "m" in "marvelous malted milk" or the "o" sound in "Go home, Joe."

Comparing and contrasting helps you to see what is the same or different about two or more ideas, objects, people, places, or anything. For example, a poet might compare an old shoe to a new shoe by listing the way the two shoes smell (stinky or fresh), look (dirty or clean), and feel (comfortable or stiff).

Concrete poems look like something you can touch. The way the poet puts the poem on the page is just as important as the words they choose. A poem about the sun might be round like the sun, or a poem about a swing might look like the words are swinging.

Couplets are pairs of rhyming lines that usually have the same number of beats. Couplets make their own point, create a separate image, or summarize the idea of a poem.

Free verse poetry is poetry that doesn't have to rhyme or stay in stanzas, or even lines. Don't let the word "free" trick you, though. The poet might use other tools to keep the poem tied together, like repeating the same sounds or words.

Haiku usually has 17 syllables (or beats) in three lines—five syllables in the first and last lines and seven in the middle. A haiku is a short poem, usually about nature and the seasons.

Imagery is what you see in your mind when you read a poem. Details like colors, sounds, sizes, shapes, comparisons, smells, and flavors all help create imagery.

Limericks are humorous poems with five lines. The last words of the first, second, and fifth lines rhyme, as do the last words of the shorter third and fourth lines. The shorter lines have two stressed beats, and the longer lines have three stressed beats.

Metaphors show how two different things are similar by calling one thing something else, such as if you call clouds "balls of cotton."

Meter measures the number of syllables, or beats, in each line of a poem. If you can count the beats, you can determine the meter. For example, some types of poems always have 10 beats per line. Others have 12.

Onomatopoeia (ON-o-MA-tow-PEE-ya) is another cool word tool that poets use. This is when the word suggests the sound or action it means, like "buzz," "hiss," and "boom."

Patterns are several things that are repeated in the same way several times. Many poems create a pattern by repeating rhyming words at the end of each line.

Personification gives human characteristics, or traits, to something that isn't human. It makes an object or animal seem human or come to life.

Repetition is what happens when poets repeat things. Repetition can help create patterns. It can also help make a point.

Rhymes are words that end in the same sound. For example, "clock" rhymes with "dock." Rhyming sounds don't have to be spelled the same way. "Pest" rhymes with "dressed."

Rhythm is the beat you can feel in poetry, like a tempo in music. Syllables, or beats, help create rhythm. Rhymes can create rhythm, too. You can measure rhythm through meter.

Similes are comparisons using "as" or "like." When you use a simile, you are saying that one thing is similar to another. Similes can help you create personification. They are also a lot like metaphors.

Stanzas are like paragraphs for poetry. They are groups of lines that sit together and are usually separated by a blank line. Sometimes a poet begins a new thought in a new stanza.

Structure is how a poem was built. A poet can build a poem using lines and stanzas.

Synonyms are words that mean almost the same thing.

Translated means that the poem was originally written in a different language.

Voice is the speaker in a poem. It can be one person, or a bunch of different people. It can be animals, objects, or even the poet.

Finding More Poetry

AT THE LIBRARY

Alarcón, Francisco X. Illustrated by Maya Christina Gonzalez. *From the Bellybutton of the Moon and Other Summer Poems.* San Francisco: Children's Book Press, 1998.

Hughes, Langston. Illustrated by Brian Pinkney. *The Dream Keeper and Other Poems.* New York: Knopf, 1994.

Kennedy, X.J. Illustrated by Joy Allen. *Exploding Gravy: Poems to Make You Laugh.* Boston: Little, Brown, 2002.

Lansky, Bruce. Illustrated by Stephen Carpenter. *If Pigs Could Fly—And Other Deep Thoughts: A Collection of Funny Poems.* Minnetonka, Minn.: Meadowbrook Press, 2000.

Shapiro, Karen Jo. Illustrated by Matt Faulkner. *Because I Could Not Stop My Bike, and Other Poems.* Watertown, Mass.: Whispering Coyote, 2003.

Silverstein, Shel. *Falling Up: Poems and Drawings.* New York: HarperCollins, 1996.

Wong, Janet S. *A Suitcase of Seaweed, and Other Poems.* New York: Margaret K. McElderry Books, 1996.

ON THE ROAD

Riley Museum

528 Lockerbie St.

Indianapolis, IN 46202

317/631-5885

To visit the historical Victorian home of poet

James Whitcomb Riley

WEB SITES

For more information on **poetry,** use FactHound
to track down Web sites related to this book.

1. Go to *www.compasspointbooks.com/facthound*

2. Type in this book ID: **0756505623**

3. Click on the FETCH IT button.

Your trusty FactHound will fetch the best Web sites for you!

ABOUT THE AUTHOR

Patricia M. Stockland has a Bachelor of Arts degree in English from South Dakota State University. She lives in Minnesota and is currently completing her Master of Arts thesis in literature from Minnesota State University, Mankato. She has taught composition and enjoys both writing and helping others write. Patricia is an editor and author of children's nonfiction books.

ABOUT THE ILLUSTRATOR

Sara Rojo Pérez was born in Madrid and now lives in Cádiz on the southern coast of Spain. For many years she worked as the creative director of an animation studio, creating both films and advertisements. Sara works in many different media—from paint in oils or acrylics to computer illustration to sculptures and tapestries. In addition to her artwork, Sara enjoys horseback riding and reading fantasy and mystery novels.

INDEX